A Little Spanish Cookbook

Carole Fahy

ILLUSTRATED BY SIMI

D0045438

First published in 1990 by
The Appletree Press Ltd, 7 James Street South,
Belfast BT2 8DL.
Copyright © 1990 The Appletree Press, Ltd. Illustrations ©
1990 Simi used under Exclusive License to
The Appletree Press, Ltd.
Printed in Hong Kong. All rights reserved.
No part of this publication may be
reproduced or transmitted in any form
or by means, electronic or mechanical,
photocopying, recording or any information
and retrieval system, without permission in
writing from the publisher

The author would like to express her grateful thanks to Anton
and Pamela Wills-Eve for their help in the preparation
of these recipes.

First published in the United States in 1990
by Chronicle Books, 275 Fifth Street,
San Francisco, CA 94103

ISBN: 0-87701-796-4

9 8 7 6 5 4 3 2 1

Introduction

A Spanish eating day centers around lunch, served late in the afternoon, eaten at a leisurely pace, and thoroughly enjoyed. Typical hors d'oeuvres are small snacks eaten with drinks. These are followed by soup, a fish or egg dish, then poultry or other meat, and vegetables. A sweet course is only served on special occasions and usually consists of pastry. Normally the meal is finished with fruit. *Tapas,* or small versions of main dishes, may be nibbled with an evening drink – perhaps at the pavement table of a bar on the famous *ramblas,* or tree-lined walks, that appear in almost every city, town, and village. Dinner, which usually does not start before 10 o'clock in the evening, is a smaller version of lunch, and breakfast may be just a cup of coffee or a glass of milk with chocolate and *churros* – strips of dough, deep-fried and coated in sugar.

Specialties vary throughout the country and each region has its own cuisine, as reflected in these recipes. Generally, however, fried foods and stews are more popular than roasts as traditionally it was customary to cook over a fire rather than in an oven. And, of course, Spain has its own wines and drinks – many types of sherry, red and white wines to suit all palates, and the cool, refreshing Sangria which is exclusive to Spain and other Spanish-speaking countries.

A note on measures
Spoon measurements are level except where otherwise indicated. Seasonings can of course be adjusted according to taste. Recipes are for four.

Entremeses y Tapas

Mixed Hors d'Oeuvres and Starters

Tapas are small, tasty, savory little snacks which are served with sherry or aperitifs. It is very easy to overeat as a wide selection are invariably placed on the table and are too appetizing to resist. The range and variety of *tapas* is enormous and the following is only a selection from the most popular:

Anchovies and sardines   These can be either fried in batter or rolled and stuffed with capers.

Calamares   Squid cut into rings and fried in batter or fried with garlic and strips of red pepper or pimento.

White fish   Pieces of white fish, fried, and chunks or flakes of canned tuna.

Shellfish and seafood   These are most commonly used in salads, with chopped onion, garlic, and oil dressing.

Biscuits   Small savory topped biscuits.

Olives   Green or black olives, usually stuffed with anchovies or pimentos.

Salads   Mixed salads of sliced or whole onions, tomatoes, red and green peppers. Rice is also often an ingredient of cold salads.

Meats and cheeses   Various cold sausages such as chorizo and butifarra and patés of all types; smoked Serrano ham is a favorite specialty; small pieces of goat's milk and other cheeses.

Nuts   A selection of nuts in shells, such as peanuts, or almonds and hazelnuts, shelled and oven-roasted.

Calderada

White Fish Soup

Excellent fish soups can be found all around the Spanish coasts. The great variety of good fresh fish gives them a succulent flavor. Served with slices of toasted crusty bread, they make a tasty starter or nourishing snack.

2 lbs white fish	3 tbsp tomato purée
1 cod's head	1 glass white wine
1 onion	1 cup milk
1 leek	few sprigs fennel
2 sticks celery	lemon peel
2 cloves garlic, finely chopped	½ cup flour
small bunch parsley	

Put the fish and vegetables into a pan. Cover with water and cook until the fish is tender. Remove carefully, taking out any bones, and cut the flesh into large pieces. Put to one side. Cook the rest of the stock for a further 20 minutes. Strain through a sieve and return to the pan. Add the white wine, tomato purée, and garlic to the stock. Blend together the flour and milk. Remove the stock from the heat and thicken with the flour and milk. Blend until the soup is smooth. Chop the parsley, fennel, and lemon peel. Add to the soup with the fish pieces. Reheat without boiling and serve immediately.

Catalan Soup

Catalan soup, like so many Spanish soups, is usually thickened with egg yolks. An equally delicious variation, which results in a thinner soup, is to omit the eggs and serve sprinkled with grated cheese.

3 large onions	2 potatoes
1/4 cup chopped ham	2 egg yolks
1 wine glass white wine	6 cups stock
1 stick celery	few sprigs thyme, chopped
3 tomatoes	few sprigs parsley, chopped
	pinch nutmeg

(serves six)

Slice the onions thinly and brown gently in a saucepan in a little olive oil. Quarter the tomatoes and chop the celery. Add them, with the ham, to the pan. Cook for a few minutes before adding the wine. Simmer gently for a few minutes. Cut the potatoes into small pieces and add to the pan with the thyme, nutmeg, and stock. Simmer gently for 30 minutes. Just before serving, beat the egg yolks together with a little of the soup. Stir well into the rest of the soup. Sprinkle with chopped parsley.

Gazpacho

Cold Vegetable Soup

This popular Andalusian dish is often called an iced soup salad. Whether it is more soup than salad depends solely on how much water is added. To give a really Spanish touch serve some of the chopped soup vegetables, together with chopped hard-boiled eggs, in separate small dishes.

4 tomatoes	1 cup fine breadcrumbs
1 small cucumber	3 tbsp oil
3 cloves garlic	2 tsp vinegar
1 onion	salt and pepper
1 red pepper	water, as required
chopped parsley (optional)	ice, as required

Mince the tomatoes, cucumber, red pepper, and onion. Crush the garlic and mix it with the salt, pepper, and breadcrumbs. Add the oil, drop by drop, to form a thick paste. Slowly stir in the vinegar and put the mixture into a soup tureen with the minced vegetables. For a thinner soup a little water can be added. Add the ice and leave the soup to stand in a cold place. Decorate with chopped parsley if desired.

Shellfish Soup

As with so many good things, a bit of time and effort—and expense—is involved in preparing this soup, but the result is well worth the effort.

I cod's head	½ cup rice
I cooked crawfish with shell	olive oil
4 cups mussels in shells	2 tbsp fresh thyme
2 cups prawns in shell	2 tbsp fresh marjoram
I pimento	2 tbsp fresh basil
I ½ lb tomatoes	2 tbsp parsley
I lemon	slice orange peel
few celery leaves	I cup white wine
I carrot	8 cups water
2 onions	I tsp saffron
2 cloves garlic	rock salt
	ground black pepper

(serves six)

Shell the crawfish and prawns. Boil up the cod's head, crawfish, and prawn shells, celery, onions, carrot, a slice of lemon, orange peel, marjoram, thyme, saffron, white wine, seasoning and water. Leave to simmer for one hour. Chop the tomatoes and simmer gently with the pimento, a clove of garlic, and a little olive oil to a purée. Strain through a sieve. Clean the mussel shells. Place in a little water over a medium heat until the shells open. Remove the mussels and strain the liquid through a fine sieve. Strain the fish and herb stock and return to the pan. Bring to a boil and add the rice. Simmer for 15 minutes. Break the crawfish into small pieces and add to the stock with the tomato purée, mussel stock, and prawns. Cook until the soup has thickened. Grate the lemon and crush the remaining clove of garlic. Add to the soup with the parsley, basil, and mussels and cook for one minute. Serve immediately.

Huevos al Plato

Baked Eggs with Ham

Eggs baked on a tasty bed of vegetables and meat make a traditional Spanish snack. Leg of pork has been used in this recipe but, if it can be obtained, any Spanish garlic sausage will give a more Iberian flavor.

---

6 eggs
4 oz cooked leg of pork
2 oz ham
3 tbsp butter
8 oz tomatoes, chopped
I tbsp flour
I onion
½ cup meat stock
(serves three)

Slice the onion. Cut the ham and pork into strips. Melt the butter in a saucepan and gently brown the onions and meat in it. Blend in the flour. Add the tomatoes and stock. Simmer gently for 20 minutes until it is very thick. Season with salt and pepper. Pour the mixture into a casserole dish. Break the eggs on top and bake in a moderate oven at 375°F until the whites have just set. Serve immediately.

Tortilla Española

Spanish Omelette

Probably the most widely eaten dish in Spain is the tortilla, or omelette, of which there are countless variations. Spaniards often claim that the French learned to make their omelettes from Spanish chefs at the court of Louis XIV after he married the daughter of Phillip IV in 1659. This recipe is a typical vegetable-based tortilla, but various cooked meats can be included.

---

3 eggs, well beaten
2 medium-sized potatoes
1 small onion
oil
salt and pepper
(serves two)

Chop the potatoes into fine matchsticks. Chop the onion. Fry these together slowly in the oil, without browning, until tender. Add the beaten eggs and fry for a couple of minutes. Now turn the omelette over to cook the other side. The easiest way to do this is to place a plate on top and turn the frying pan upside down, then slip the tortilla back into the pan on the other side.

Sardinas Fritas

Grilled Sardines

The differing sizes of Spanish sardines makes them a versatile fish for cooking. The smaller ones, cooked straight from the sea, are served as *tapas* with a cold beer in all the little coastal bars. The larger ones, served with salad and fresh crusty bread, make a good main course. The recipe is simple but the result is a treat.

8 large sardines
salt
olive oil

Slit the sardines from head to tail and clean thoroughly. Salt lightly. Brush both sides with a little oil and grill or fry for a few minutes until a crisp golden-brown on both sides. Serve immediately.

Calamares en su Tinta

Squid in Its Own Ink

Beautiful purple *calamares* can be found all along the Mediterranean coast and are considered a great delicacy. Squid is obtainable in many parts of the world, making this unusual Spanish dish available to everybody. It is best when served with saffron rice.

2 lb squid	1 tbsp chopped parsley
1 large onion	1/3 cup white wine
2 cloves garlic	2 tbsp dry breadcrumbs
2 tbsp olive oil	salt and pepper
2 tomatoes	

To clean the squid separate the sac from the head and cut off the tentacles. Remove the gristle and the bag containing the ink from the sac. Put the ink bag to one side. Thoroughly wash the tentacles and the sac, inside and out. Slice the sac into rings and cut the tentacles into pieces. Peel and slice the tomatoes. Chop the onion and the garlic. Cook the tomatoes, onion, and garlic in the olive oil for a few minutes. Add the squid, wine, a little water, parsley, salt, and pepper. Cover and simmer gently for about 30 minutes. Stir in the liquid from the ink bag and thicken with the breadcrumbs.

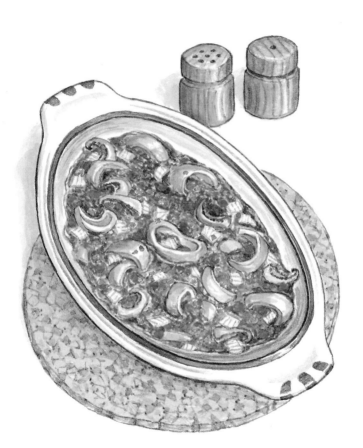

Raya en Pimenton

Skate in Red Pepper

The only edible parts of the skate are the 'wings', or side parts. The tastiest and most tender are from small young skate which are usually sold whole. This southern Spanish dish is both inexpensive and easy to prepare, and makes a mouth-watering meal.

2¼ lb skate
4 cloves garlic
1 sprig parsley
olive oil
1 tsp paprika
1 tsp saffron
1 tsp chopped marjoram

Place the skate in a large, greased casserole dish. Lightly fry all the other ingredients in the olive oil then grind them down in a mortar. Spread this mixture over the fish and cook in a moderate oven at 350°F for about 30 minutes.

Arroz Marinera

Seafood with Rice

Rice is such a popular ingredient in all types of Spanish cooking that there are many seafood-with-rice dishes. This one comes from a little restaurant at Torredembarra near Valencia. If angler fish is not available, any firm white fish can be substituted.

2 cups rice	2 cloves garlic, chopped
8 oz squid, cleaned	8 oz onions, chopped
8 oz cuttlefish, cleaned	12 oz tomatoes
12 oz angler fish	8 oz (shelled weight) green
8 oz prawns	peas
18 mussels	1 red pepper
6 clams	cooking oil
	salt and pepper

(serves six)

Thoroughly clean the mussel and clam shells. Heat some oil in a large saucepan and cook the mussels and clams until they open, then remove from the shells. Add the garlic and onion to the mussels and clams in the pan and cook for a few minutes. Chop the cleaned squid and cuttlefish into small pieces. Add these and the tomatoes to the pan and cook for ten minutes. Add the rice and cook for a few minutes, making sure the rice is just covered by the oil. Add 1 1/3 cups boiling water, the angler fish and prawns. Season with salt and pepper. Add the peas and strips of red pepper. Bring to a boil and simmer for 20 minutes. Leave to settle for five minutes before serving.

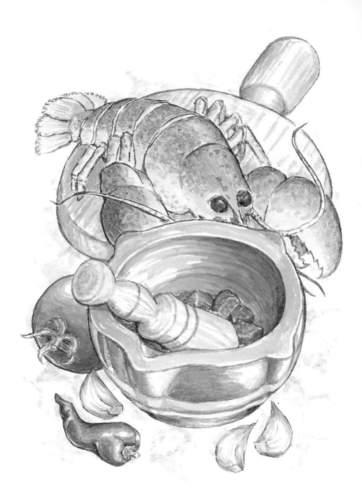

Lobster Romesco

Freshly caught shellfish is the most common luxury in Spanish cuisine. The tangy sauce, which gives this dish its name, is delicious with either hot or cold cooked lobster.

2 cooked lobsters	1 tbsp paprika
2 tomatoes	salt
1 red chili	2 tbsp olive oil
1 clove of garlic	vinegar

To prepare the lobster twist off the large claws and crack them without damaging the flesh. Remove and discard the smaller claws and the head. Using a sharp pointed knife split the lobster down the middle of the body from head to tail. Remove and discard the intestines, stomach, and gills. Arrange the body and large claws on a serving dish. To make the sauce put the tomatoes, chili, and garlic into a moderate oven for a few minutes until soft but not browned. Skin the tomatoes and garlic. Skin and seed the chili. Pound them together in a mortar. Add the salt and paprika. Mix in the olive oil, add a little vinegar if necessary, but keep the sauce thick. Press the sauce through a fine sieve and serve with the lobster.

Paella de Mariscos

Fish Paella

This traditional rice dish can be made with either meat or fish and sometimes has both, but the two main ingredients are always rice and saffron. It is often served in the large, shallow pan in which it is cooked. The Spanish paella pan has two loop handles and is made of aluminium, heavy iron, or earthenware. However, a large heavy frying pan about 12 in. in diameter serves just as well.

1 medium sized crayfish, cooked and cut in pieces	*2 cloves garlic*
6 large shrimp	*1 onion, chopped*
1 lb angler fish cut in pieces	*1 cup rice*
6 small ink fish	*1 tsp red pepper*
4 tomatoes, skinned and seeded	*1 tsp saffron*
	fish stock
	oil for frying

(serves 6)

Fry all the fish in the oil and garlic. Just before it is cooked, add the onion and tomato. Stir in the rice and cook for a few minutes. Add just enough hot fish stock to cover the rice. Add salt, pepper and saffron and simmer until the rice is thoroughly cooked.

À Little Spanish Cookbook

Carole Fahy

ILLUSTRATED BY SIMI

Entremeses y Tapas

Mixed Hors d'Oeuvres and Starters

Tapas are small, tasty, savory, little snacks which are served with sherry or aperitifs. It is very easy to overeat as a wide selection are invariably placed on the table and are too appetizing to resist. The range and variety of *tapas* is enormous and the following is only a selection from the most popular:

Anchovies and sardines These can be either fried in batter or rolled and stuffed with capers.

Calamares Squid cut into rings and fried in batter or fried with garlic and strips of red pepper or pimento.

White fish Pieces of white fish, fried, and chunks or flakes of canned tuna.

Shellfish and seafood These are most commonly used in salads, with chopped onion, garlic, and oil dressing.

Biscuits Small savory topped biscuits.

Olives Green or black olives, usually stuffed with anchovies or pimentos.

Salads Mixed salads of sliced or whole onions, tomatoes, red and green peppers. Rice is also often an ingredient of cold salads.

Chronicle

Paella Valenciana

Chicken Paella

1 medium-sized chicken	1 tsp paprika
½ cup cooking oil	1½ cups rice
8 slices lean bacon	4 cups hot water
1 tomato, peeled and chopped	pinch saffron
1 clove garlic, chopped	salt
8 oz French beans	12 snails (optional)
2 leaf artichokes	

Cut the chicken into 14 pieces. Salt it. Cut the bacon into small pieces. Heat the oil in a flame-proof casserole and fry the chicken and bacon for five minutes. Add the tomato, garlic, beans, artichokes, paprika, rice, saffron, and water. Bring to a boil and add the snails if required. Season to taste, and simmer gently for 20 minutes. Serve from the pan.

Chuletas a la Parilla con Ali~Oli

Lamb Chops with Ali-Oli Sauce

Ali-Oli is a popular Spanish garlic mayonnaise. Do not spoil it by trying to prepare it too quickly. Take care to add the oil drop by drop, stirring continuously to make a thick, smooth cream. The strong garlic flavor goes especially well with lamb.

---

4 large lamb chops
15 cloves garlic
2 cups olive oil
juice of 1/4 lemon
2 egg yolks
salt

As the sauce is served cold it can be prepared in advance. Crush the garlic in a bowl. Gradually beat together the garlic and enough oil to form a smooth paste. Beat in the egg yolks and then the remaining oil, drop by drop. Stir in the lemon juice and salt. Put to one side. Lightly salt the chops. Brush with a little oil and grill for a few minutes each side. Lamb tastes better if left pink in the center when serving with a garlic sauce. Serve hot, with the sauce in a separate dish.

Pote Gallego

Galician Stew

Spanish beef can be rather tough and so it tends to be cooked slowly in a stew. It is usual with a meat and vegetable stew to drain the liquid off and use this as a soup. The meat and vegetables can then be eaten as the main course–an easy way of cooking two courses at once!

1 lb stewing steak
4 oz lean ham, chopped
2 oz lean bacon, chopped
4 oz chorizo (Spanish garlic sausage), sliced
4 oz Morcilla (black pudding), sliced
2 cups dried haricot beans
1 white cabbage, chopped
2 lb potatoes

Cut the steak into large pieces. Put two pints of cold water into a saucepan. Add the meats. Season to taste and simmer gently over a low heat. Cook the beans and white cabbage in a separate pan until they are tender. Add to the meat, then add the potatoes and bring to a boil. Simmer gently until the potatoes are cooked. Strain off the liquid to use as a soup. Serve the vegetables, meat, and potatoes as the main course.

Cazuela Catalana

Catalan Stew

This is a delicious mixture of beef and sausage from Catalonia.

---

2 lb minced beef
8 oz butifarra (Spanish pork sausage), sliced
2 onions, chopped
cooking oil
2 tomatoes, chopped
2 carrots, chopped
1 tbsp flour
stock
(serves 6)

Heat oil in a flame-proof casserole dish and fry the mince until it is just cooked, then remove it. Fry the carrots, onions, and tomatoes in the same pan for a few minutes. Stir continuously to prevent sticking. Blend in the flour and cook for a few more minutes. Add the cooked mince. Cover with hot stock and simmer gently for about 45 minutes. If necessary add more hot stock. When cooked, arrange the slices of butifarra around the edge of the casserole and heat in a hot oven at 400°F.

Arroz Catalana

Sausage and Rice Casserole

A typical meat and fish mixture forms the basis of this substantial casserole. It is ideal for a cold winter's evening.

1 cup rice	1 squid
3 oz chorizo (garlic sausage)	12 mussels, cooked and
2 oz uncooked pork	shelled
2 oz pork fat	1 oz almonds
2 tomatoes	1 oz pine kernels
8 oz peas	2 cloves garlic
2 leaf artichokes	1 onion
2 red peppers	pinch saffron
	parsley

Slice the onion and garlic sausage. Cut the pork into small pieces. Wash and slice the red peppers and tomatoes. Clean the squid and cut the flesh into small pieces. Remove the outer leaves of the artichokes and quarter the hearts. Melt the pork fat in a flame-proof casserole dish and fry the pork, garlic sausage, and onion in it for a few minutes. Add the red pepper, tomato, and squid. Cook gently for 15 minutes. Add the peas, rice, artichokes, mussels, almonds, and pine kernels, garlic, saffron, and 4 cups boiling water. Simmer gently until the rice has cooked. Garnish with parsley and serve from the casserole dish.

Ternera Asada

Pot Roast Veal

In Spain, calves are not killed when very young, so veal is an older meat which resembles British beef. This makes it a good meat for pot roasting. When cooked on top of the cooker, the joint can be served with a potato purée and selection of vegetables.

2¼ lb veal
2 tbsp oil
I wine glass white wine
I onion, chopped
salt and pepper

Seal the meat in hot oil in a flame-proof casserole dish. Add the wine, onion, and seasoning. Cover the casserole dish and cook on a low heat slowly for two hours. Remove the meat and thicken the juices to make a gravy.

Cazuela

Vegetable Casserole

This dish serves as a light snack or a side dish to a main meat course.
It is sometimes considered the Spanish equivalent of ratatouille.

2¼ lb broad beans	10 small leaf artichokes
4 onions, finely chopped	1 tsp chopped mint
2 cloves garlic, chopped	1 tsp saffron
cooking oil	½ tsp cumin
2 tomatoes, chopped	½ tsp white pepper
1 bay leaf	1 slice fried bread
1 tsp chopped parsley	6 eggs
1 tsp chopped mint	

(serves 6)

Shell the beans. Cover with cold water and bring to a boil. Simmer
gently until half-cooked. Drain. Fry the garlic and onions together in
oil until brown. Add the tomatoes and the partly-cooked beans.
Just cover with boiling water. Add the herbs and artichokes. Cover
and simmer gently until the beans are soft. Stir in the saffron, cumin,
and pepper. Crumble in the fried bread. Pour the mixture into a
casserole dish and break the eggs into it. Cook in a preheated oven
at 375°F until the eggs are cooked.

Pimientos Verdes Rellenos

Stuffed Green Peppers

There are many different ways of serving stuffed peppers. In a country where tomatoes are plentiful, tomato sauce is made fresh, and the result is a dish to be savored either as an entrée or a light snack.

4 green peppers	4 tsp cooking oil
3 cloves garlic, chopped	6 tsp Worcester sauce
3 tsp mixed herbs	3 beaten eggs

Tomato sauce

2 tbsp chopped onion	½ tsp chopped basil
cooking oil	I bay leaf
I lb tomatoes	½ tsp sugar
½ tsp chopped parsley	salt and pepper

Mix together the garlic, mixed herbs, Worcester sauce, and eggs. Heat the oil and slowly fry the mixture. Halve the peppers lengthways. Remove the stalks and seeds and wash well. Blanch in boiling salted water. Drain and fill with the mixture. Arrange in a greased casserole dish. To make the sauce, soften the onion in a little oil without browning. Quarter the tomatoes and add to the onions. Add the herbs, sugar, salt, and pepper. Simmer gently to a pulp. Strain through a sieve and make up to 2 cups with hot water. Pour the sauce over the peppers. Cook in a low oven at 350°F for 20 minutes.

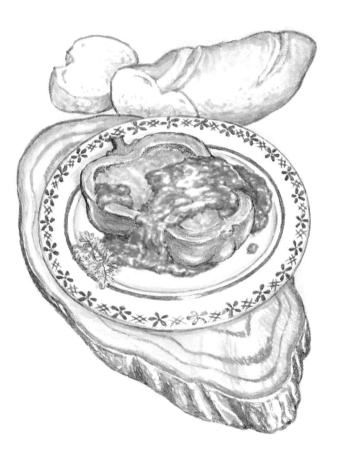

Olla Cordobesa

Cordova Stew

This chick-pea stew is one which traces its origins back to the Arab occupation of southern Spain more than a thousand years ago. It does take some time to prepare and cook. The chick-peas available in England usually take a bit longer to cook than this recipe suggests, sometimes as long as five hours.

4½ cups chick-peas
8 oz tocino (fat bacon)
I lb white cabbage, chopped
4 cups boiling salted water

Soak the chick-peas for at least 12 hours and drain. Pour boiling water over them. Leave to stand in this water for about five minutes and then drain. Place in a pan with the boiling salted water. Simmer for one hour and then add the fat bacon. Simmer for a further 30 minutes and add the cabbage. Simmer for another 30 minutes or until the chick-peas are cooked.

Pipirrana

Green Salad with Ham

For a really refreshing meal in summer, place the bowl of salad inside a larger bowl which has been lined with ice cubes and leave in a refrigerator for a few hours before serving.

2¼ lbs tomatoes
3 green peppers
4 hard-boiled eggs
3 oz canned bonito or tuna
4 cloves garlic
I tbsp olive oil
I slice bread, without crust
½ tsp salt
I tbsp vinegar
Serrano ham

Soak the bread in a little water. Scald, skin, seed, and chop the tomatoes. Grill the peppers lightly, then peel and chop them. Chop the egg whites. Drain the canned fish and flake with a fork. Make a dressing by crushing together the garlic, egg yolks, oil, and softened bread. Mix well. Add the salt and vinegar. Put all the salad ingredients into a salad bowl with the fish. Pour the dressing over them. Chill in the refrigerator. Serve with slices of Serrano ham.

Tortas de Aceite

Aniseed Biscuits

This is one of a great variety of little cakes and biscuits that are eaten throughout Spain. Whenever a cup of coffee or a glass of sherry is drunk, a selection of biscuits is sure to be offered.

2 cups flour
2/3 cup sugar
2 tbsp oil
1 egg
1 liquer glass dry anis
grated rind of one lemon
1/2 tsp salt

Mix together the flour, sugar, salt and grated lemon rind. Make a well in the center and pour in the beaten egg, oil, and anis. Gradually stir all the ingredients together to give a smooth, firm mixture. Roll this out thinly and cut into small rounds. Place on a greased baking tray and cook in a preheated hot oven at 425°F for ten minutes. The number of biscuits made will depend on how thinly the mixture is rolled out.

Torrijas

Sherry Bread Pudding

This sweet but spicy syrup pudding is the Spanish way of using up stale bread.

2/3 cup sugar
8 slices white bread about 1/4 in thick
pinch cinnamon
small glass sherry
1/2 cup water
small piece lemon peel
1 cup milk
1 large egg
olive oil

Prepare a syrup by heating together the sugar, water, lemon peel, and cinnamon for about ten minutes. Leave to cool and then add the sherry. Soak the bread in milk and then dip in the beaten egg. Fry the bread in very hot oil until golden and crisp. Pour the cold syrup over the bread and serve immediately.

Sopa Inglesa

Trifle

Literally translated this means English soup. This dessert, however, is anything but a soup. Similar to the English trifle, but richer and creamier, it is ideal for special occasions.

---

1 sponge cake
1/2 cup sherry
1 cup whipping cream
12 oz strawberries, fresh or canned
a little sugar
a few crystallized fruits

Split the sponge cake in half. Cut one half into medium-size pieces and arrange on the base of a large trifle dish. Pour half the sherry over them and leave to stand for one hour. Cut the other half of the sponge into pieces and leave to stand in the rest of the sherry. Hull and wash fresh strawberries and sprinkle with a little sugar. Strain canned strawberries, if used. Whip the cream until firm. Arrange the strawberries on top of the sponge in the dish and cover with half the cream. Carefully place the rest of the sherry-soaked sponge on top of the cream. Arrange the remaining strawberries on top of this and cover with the rest of the cream. Chill in the refrigerator for a couple of hours. Just before serving, decorate with a few crystallized fruits.

Gachas

Cadiz Custard

This unusual dessert from Cadiz resembles porridge and, like porridge, is served piping hot with a variety of toppings—sugar, milk, honey, syrup—according to taste.

---

3 tbsp oil
1 tsp anis seeds
2 tbsp flour
1 cup boiling water

Fry the anis seeds in oil for 15 minutes. Strain the oil into another pan and blend in the flour. Stir continuously until the mixture bubbles. Do not allow to brown. Add the boiling water and beat well. Simmer gently until it thickens to the consistency of baked custard. Serve immediately.

Sangria

Every visitor to Spain is glad that such delicious, cool wine and fruit cups are drunk throughout the country. Sangria can be made with varying alcoholic strengths and a variety of recipes, but invariably the basis of the recipe is a combination of fresh fruit and wine. A typical Sangria should have at least some fresh peaches, lemons, oranges and apples. These are sliced and placed in a large, specially-lipped jug, and a bottle of local red wine poured over the slices. Ice cubes and soda water or lemonade are added to top up the jug. The quantity of liquid determines the strength of the cup. The spices normally used in punch, especially cinnamon, are often added to give a tangy bite. The best Sangria is always homemade, but it can be bought ready-mixed.

Index